TERRAFORMING THE  CLOUD

Satish Balakrishnan

WhiteFalcon
Publishing

www.whitefalconpublishing.com

Terraforming The Cloud
Satish Balakrishnan

www.whitefalconpublishing.com

Requests for permission should be addressed to
xsatishx@gmail.com

ISBN - 978-1-63640-155-3

This Book is dedicated to my parents, Mr Balakrishnan and Ms Padma Balakrishnan for making me who I am today, my wife Ms Madhumati Satish for encouraging me and supporting me in this journey and my loving daughter, Yuti Satish who has been my lucky charm.

Contents

Foreword

Who can use this book?

This book is a beginners guide to Terraform. The book is for anyone who wishes to get started with Terraform and learn more about it. The people who will be most benefitted out of this book are the students who wish to pursue a career in infrastructure and cloud computing. This book is certainly not for the terraform experts out there.

This book uses many Amazon Web Services terminologies and Jargons, so it is expected that the reader is aware of these concepts along with a basic understanding of Linux.

Having an Amazon Web Services account will help the readers to do some hands-on exercises, however this is not mandatory. Amazon Web Services provides a free usage tier which should be more than enough to start with. You still need a credit card to access the free tier. You may or may not be charged depending on your usage.

Some of the code snippets work on terraform v0.11. The snippets give an idea and may not work if you try to copy and paste it directly. The reader should understand the concepts and then recreate the later versions' configuration codes without any issues.

Cloud

## CHAPTER ONE

All about the Cloud

Cloud is everywhere. During the last few years, every industry known to humanity has been shifting towards cloud computing and leveraging the fantastic benefits. Just like 'google' has become a synonym for search, 'cloud' has become a synonym for infrastructure and applications in general. The root of most technological innovation is the computing power behind it and recently, various cloud providers' computing power. To understand how 'cloud' started its dominance, it is essential to understand the ecosystem before cloud computing. System administrators maintain servers which include hardware, software, operating system and networking. If something goes wrong, then it would take weeks to get it operational again. Having a backup server would incur as much cost and even with the backup server, the time consumed for failover is significant. When a storage server runs out of space, the only option is to purchase new storage disks and then configure it, which could be expensive and time-consuming.

Mainframe computers were very similar to what cloud computing offers now because they provided a massive infrastructure for applications; however, setting up mainframes requires enormous up-front investments. Add to it the cost of maintenance and repairs, and you can imagine how the costs escalate rapidly. With cloud computing, all the infrastructure is managed by the service provider. They have multiple data centres in different regions or countries to cater to high availability and reduce latency. Virtualisation practically changed the landscape of how IT and Technology companies operate. It became possible to deftly scale up and scale down, terminate and spawn servers and storage devices. Companies could spin up new servers without having to own a data centre and manage the underlying hardware. It is also possible to spin up non-production environments with the same configuration as production environments and test it thoroughly. If, at any point, any of the environment breaks, you can spin up a new environment within minutes thanks to Infrastructure as Code (IaC). The latest buzz word is on-demand technology which essentially implies that you can get servers, storage, network, compute etc. without actually placing an order, waiting for it to be delivered and assembling it.

Early years of the century saw the rise of Amazon Web Services encompassing three services - EC2 (compute engine), S3 (object storage) and SQS (messaging queue service). Amazon realised that they were using less than 15% of their capacity and decided to address this problem, resulting in Amazon Web Services. AWS started gaining popularity quickly, which resulted in other big players entering the market with Microsoft launching Azure and Google launching Google cloud platform. AWS, Google and Microsoft own a significant chunk in the public cloud sector followed by others like Alibaba, Oracle and IBM. Due to specific reasons like costs or features, many organisations prefer to use certain services with one cloud provider while maintaining other cloud providers' services. Multi-cloud strategies are popular with technology startups. There are other reasons like data governance for which some organisations tend to keep specific workloads on-premise while using the public cloud for the other services. Hybrid cloud strategies are getting adopted more and more by more prominent organisations and enterprises. With so many cloud providers in the market and many more in the private cloud space, it becomes tough to provision resources in all of these while maintaining and following standard policies and rules.

While AWS has been dominating in terms of market share, Microsoft Azure is not far behind. Azure is much more attractive for enterprise customers as they usually use Microsoft products. With Azure stack, they even extend the cloud usage to the on-premise world. AWS has outposts that allow you to implement AWS on-prem. Google has something interesting, their hybrid cloud approach is all about Kubernetes, and it is called Anthos. More and more companies are adopting container technologies in the recent past, reducing server costs and increasing efficiency. It allows you to package your applications into a standardised unit for development, shipment and deployment. They are lightweight and isolate the application from its environment, allowing the application to be independent of additional factors and underlying infrastructure. This probably is one of the reasons why Google is banking on Kubernetes for its hybrid solution. Kubernetes is a container orchestration platform that makes running containers easy, allowing you to efficiently scale applications and optimise infrastructure resources.

Generally, while developing software, the developers use a version control system like git or svn to record changes to a set of codes that occur during the Software development life cycle. By versioning their code, they make sure that they can go back to a previous version. What if such a feature was available to manage all your infrastructure. You write your infrastructure as code, version it, and then run it to create the resources. You can provision resources across multiple cloud providers. That's precisely what HashiCorp's Terraform does. As cool as the name sounds, you will be amazed by what it can achieve.

## CHAPTER TWO

Public Cloud Vs Private Cloud

When you talk about cloud, it merely means that you have a set of hardware in a data centre, and all the users share this set of hardware for their workloads, and once done, they can release it into the pool again. Other users can start using the hardware that is available in the collection. Of course, security standards are very high, and even if the hardware is shared, the data between is never shared or visible to others. The above feature is what makes the cloud so popular.

A private cloud is when you have the entire cloud (hardware) in your data centre and manage it. Again the resources are provisioned and de-provisioned based on the usage. The private cloud can help you address some compliance-related specifics but require you to do the heavy lifting. On the other hand, the public cloud is managed by companies like Amazon, Google, Microsoft, etc., and is located around the world in the massive data centre. They also provide you with certain managed services like database, container orchestration, etc., which means you are just going to use them and pay for it based on usage. The difference is also between Opex and Capex.

With the public cloud, maintaining infrastructure and service stability such as backups, disaster recovery, or updates are held with the providers. At the same time, the application layer security is still a user responsibility and understandably so.

Amazon Web Services or AWS is a set of services and tools that are reliable, scalable, and cost-effective. They use distributed IT infrastructure to make resources available on demand. Amazon owns data centres worldwide, and then they provide them to their customers by virtualising them. The customers or users of AWS no longer need to maintain and hold a datacenter. Most of these services are billed peruse, which means that you don't have to pay for something that you have stopped using temporarily. They also offer certain managed services to maintain the servers to use without worrying about the upgrades and operations. Flexibility is a significant benefit that one can make use of as soon as you begin your journey with AWS. Combine that with the pay per use model; it gives organisations a massive benefit in agility and costs. Below is a non-exhaustive comparison between the public and private cloud.

Situations when public clouds are useful:

- You have reasonably diverse computing needs and requirements.
- Your services are needed by a business that has apresence across the world or the region.
- Frequent needs of burst computing and on demand compute and storage requirements.
- You are looking to host your Non-production environments like development and test environments to shut them off when not in use.

Benefits of using public cloud

- With public cloud, you can shift your financial model from Capex to Opex.
- You can achieve high scalability and ability to handle sudden spikes in infrastructure requirements.
- Repurpose and reskill your IT staff to gain agility.
- You can choose to pay only for what you use and avoid over purchasing of hardware.
- Since the pricing is agile, it gives you an option to switch strategies based on the current market situation.

Limitations of public cloud

- The cost can significantly increase if the architecture is not up to the mark.
- Since the provider manages the infrastructure, there is a lack of control and visibility.

Situations when private clouds are useful:

- Highly-regulated industries and government or quasi-government organisations.
- Technology companies that need to control their infrastructure.
- Large companies that have significant infrastructure requirements.

Benefits of using private cloud

- Dedicated and secure environments that can only be accessed within the organisation.

- Compliance with customised and strict protocols depending on the workload.
- Ability to transform the infrastructure based on the business and IT needs of the organisation.

Limitations of private cloud

- The high cost of ownership and maintenance.
- If the infrastructure needs to be scaled, significant time, money, and efforts are required.

## CHAPTER THREE

Public Cloud Providers

Today's three leading public cloud providers are Amazon Web Services (AWS), Microsoft Azure, and Google Cloud. Other players are who are catching up slowly. The Gartner magic quadrant is a good indicator of the standings of these cloud providers.

Gartner's Magic Quadrant for Public cloud (2019)

AWS is the market leader and was started in 2006. AWS has more than 190 services and products across compute, storage, database, analytics, networking, mobile, developer tools, management tools, IoT, security, and enterprise applications. Microsoft Azure started around 2010 and is the clear favourite among C-suite executives as they have a long-standing relationship even before the cloud began. Azure has more than 100 services. Google entered the race in 2013 and stood out for its deep expertise around open source technologies, especially containers, Kubernetes for orchestration, and the Istio service mesh, quickly becoming industry-standard technologies. Google has more than 70 services.

While AWS has been dominating in terms of market share, Microsoft Azure is not far behind. Azure is much more attractive for enterprise customers as they usually have some Microsoft products already within their environment and hence an established relationship with Microsoft. With Azure stack, they even extend the cloud usage to on-premise. This encourages organisations and enterprises to have their sensitive data and workloads running on-premise and everything else on the cloud. This approach is also known as a hybrid cloud. AWS launched its hybrid cloud solution called 'outpost' in the last quarter of 2019. Google's hybrid cloud approach is interesting, focusing on Kubernetes and called 'Anthos.' More and more companies are adopting the container technologies in the recent past, which reduces server costs and increases efficiency. It allows you to package your applications into standardised units for development, shipment, and deployment. They are lightweight and isolate the application from its environment. This allows the application run to be the same, always irrespective of the underlying infrastructure. This is one of the reasons why Google is banking on Kubernetes for its hybrid solution.

Pricing plays a crucial role in attracting customers, considering a move to the cloud. Over the years, there has been a continuous downtrend in prices from all the three major cloud providers, mainly due to competition. Overall, the prices are comparable now ever since AWS shifted from per-hour pricing to per-second pricing for its EC2 services, which Azure and Google already had. It's tough to make an exact comparison as they have different pricing models, discounts, and services on offer. All three clouds provide a pricing calculator that can help make the decision initially.

The pricing calculator URL for the three major services providers is below.

- AWS

  https://calculator.aws/

- Azure

  https://azure.microsoft.com/pricing/calculator/

- Google

  https://cloud.google.com/products/calculator/

Let's talk about some of the essential services that AWS offers.

EC2 (Elastic Cloud Compute) - Virtual servers in the cloud with plenty of options to choose from RAM and CPU's varying capacity. You are provided with preconfigured templates and also combinations of RAM and CPU that you can select. Within a couple of minutes, the entirely usable virtual machine will be ready for you to use. You can also choose these virtual machines or instances in any region where AWS has a datacenter.

S3 (Simple Storage Service)- Scalable object storage on the cloud offers scalability, data availability, security, and performance. It can store data for various use cases such as websites, mobile applications, backup, archive, IoT devices, storing images, and big data analytics.

EKS (Elastic Kubernetes Service) - Managed Kubernetes service that lets you orchestrate containers.

Kubernetes is a container orchestration platform that automates much manual work that you need to do otherwise. Essentially they have master nodes (machines that have all the control plane tools installed) and worker nodes (devices where your workload runs). AWS manages the master nodes for you and lets you manage what matters the most - your workloads. You can spin up a Kubernetes cluster within 5 minutes.

Elastic Beanstalk- Elastic Beanstalk is a compute service that makes it easier for the developers to deploy and manage applications you upload to the AWS cloud. Beanstalk allows developers to upload their application as a zip file, and then Beanstalk provisions and handle the configuration on your behalf. The application will be provided with capacity provisioning, load balancing, auto-scaling, and health monitoring. This form of compute service is also known as Platform as a Service (Paas)

Lambda - Run your code in response to events without servers. AWS Lambda lets you run code without provisioning or managing servers. You pay only for the computing time you consume. With Lambda, you can run code for virtually any type of application or backend service. All you need to do is upload your code and let Lambda manage everything else, including high availability.

Aurora - Aurora is a high performance and managed relational database system. It is compatible with MySQL and PostgreSQL and is built for the cloud. Amazon claims that it is up to five times faster than standard MySQL databases and three times faster than standard PostgreSQL databases. Aurora's key features are that it is a distributed and fault-tolerant database with a self-healing storage system.

DynamoDB - Amazon DynamoDB is a fully managed NoSQL database service that is simple and cost-effective to store and retrieve any data and serve any request traffic level. It provides fast and predictable performance with seamless scalability. According to Amazon, DynamoDB can handle more than 10 trillion requests per day and can support peaks of more than 20 million requests per second.

VPC (Virtual Private Cloud)- Amazon Virtual Private Cloud lets you provision a logically isolated section of the AWS Cloud where you can launch AWS resources in a virtual network that you define. Simply put, you can consider it as a separate virtual data center to manage your resources.

Amazon Sagemaker - Amazon SageMaker is a fully managed service that provides the ability to build, train, and deploy machine learning models quickly. SageMaker removes the heavy lifting from each step of the machine learning process to make it easier to develop high-quality models.

These are some of the services that AWS offers. Since there are around 200 services that AWS offers and the list keeps growing, it is out of this book's scope to cover every one of them. The below table displays frequently used services and the names given by the three cloud providers.

Service \ Cloud Provider	AWS	Azure	GCP
Virtual Servers	Elastic Compute Cloud	Virtual Machine	Compute Engine
PaaS	Elastic Beantask	Cloud Services	App Engine
Kubernetes	Elastic Kubernetes Service	Azure Kubernetes Service	Kubernetes Engine
Serverless	AWS Lambda	Azure Functions	GCP Functions
Object Storage	Simple Storage Service	Storage	Google Cloud Storage
Block Storage	Elastic Block Store	Azure Disk Storage	Google Persistent Disk
File Storage	Elastic File System	Azure Files	Google Cloud Filestore
Custom Database	Amazon Aurora	Azure Cosmos DB	Cloud Spanner
Relational Database	RDS	SQL database	Cloud Spanner/SQL
NoSQL	DynamoDB	Azure Cosmos DB	Google Cloud Bigtable
Dataware house	Amazon Redshit	SQL Data Warehouse	Google Cloud BigQuery
Security Assessment	Amazon Inspector	Azure Security Center	Cloud Security Command Center
Threat Detection	Amazon GuardDuty	Azure Security and Compliance	Cloud Armor
Virtual Private Cloud	Amazon VPC	Virtual Network	Google VPC
Load Balancing	Elastic Load Balancer	Azure Load Balancer	Cloud load Balancer
Machine Learning	SageMaker	Machine Learning	Cloud Machine Learning Engine
GIT repositories	CodeCommit	Source Repositories	Cloud Source Repositories
Authentication	IAM	Active Directory	Cloud IAM
API Management	API Gateway	Cloud Endpoints	API Management

A subset of services offered by the three cloud providers and the names that they are known by

DevOps

## CHAPTER FOUR

All about DevOps

Back in the day, the server management room used to be occupied by several engineers, monitoring the servers 24 hours a day to ensure that the business runs without any trouble. With cloud service providers' arrival, you don't need to be physically present in the server management rooms. If you have your processes properly setup, you may not even need anyone monitoring it full time. The time is taken to set up and provision a server has drastically reduced so much that people can now do it on demand, thanks to DevOps. DevOps is a concept that incorporates technological tools or methods and recommends changes in terms of people and how they operate, and the organization's overall culture. With an idea of improving and optimizing an organization's ability to deliver its products or services. It is a growing trend that combines software development and information technology operations with agility and collaboration.

DevOps enabled; generally, the development and operations teams have to move out of the siloed approach and work as a single unit. This team has to work across the entire software development lifecycle, from development to test, to deployed to operations and maintenance. In some cases, the testing team or the quality assurance team and the security team may work together or work as part of the development and operations team throughout the application lifecycle. Such practices may also be known as DevSecOps.

Organizations that adopt the DevOps model use a combination of suitable and chosen technological solutions and multiple tooling to help them operate and release applications at a faster pace while still being reliable. Some of these tools can complement the engineers and enable them to independently accomplish tasks like deploying code or provisioning infrastructure that normally would have required help from other teams. The tools used while embracing the DevOps culture may fit into one of the following criteria.

- Developing the Code
- Building the Code
- Testing the code
- Packaging the code
- Releasing the package
- Configuring the infrastructure
- Monitoring
- Security

## CHAPTER FIVE

DevOps Practices

DevOps, as we can see, enables organizations to deliver high-quality products, improve time to market, boost productivity, reduce operational cost, and stay competitive in the market. DevOps provides a variety of principles and practices. Following are some of the best practices following which enables an organization to adopt the DevOps framework. While all of these are not mandatory, adopting these would allow an organization to be highly agile and efficient.

1. Test Automation

To ensure high quality, the developers have to test the software regularly. Under the DevOps framework, it is highly recommended to try as early in the SDLC as possible, giving the developers ample time and opportunity to resolve issues. Automated testing works perfectly in such a scenario and speeds up the software delivery timeline. Test automation can be applied to configurations made to Database, Network, Application, Middleware. It can be part of sanity testing, regression testing, and/on load testing. To compose quality code, developers need to test the software regularly. DevOps allows for early testing that enables developers to identify and resolve the issue during software development rather than later in the process. To have a complete and successful test automation process, it is crucial to determine the test scenarios, choose the right automation tools, setting up an automation environment in a repeatable manner, executing the test, and analyzing results.

2. Continuous Integration

Continuous Integration enables developers to integrate their code into a version control system as often as possible. Usually, the codes are checked in every day. As soon as the code is checked in, a new build is triggered, and tests are carried out against the build. The whole idea is to fail fast and fail quickly so that the amount of debugging is limited to a day's code in this case. CI tools help to detect the integration challenges in new and existing code at a very early stage.

3. Continuous Delivery

Continuous delivery picks up where continuous integration ends. Continuous delivery takes the application (or any form of the application) and then moves it to a selected environment. Generally, as part of its SDLC, every organization has multiple environments like development, UAT, Pre-production other than the production environment. Continuous delivery automates the pushing of code to these environments.

4. Continuous Deployment

Once a company adopts CI/CD methodologies and fine-tunes their Continous Integration and Delivery, they can then opt to implement continuous deployment where application changes run through the CI/CD pipeline and passing builds are deployed directly to production environments. With continuous deployment, enabled development is faster as there is no need to pause releases. Deployments pipelines are triggered automatically for every change that happens.

5 . Infrastructure as Code

Another important process in DevOps is Infrastructure as Code, where you manage your infrastructure and all its components in a definition file. The definition file can be stored in a version control system of your choice. This allowed infrastructure operators to bake software best practices into a code and uniformly use the same tool with multiple infrastructures. The developers guaranteed that the infrastructure would be the same always as it does away with the error-prone aspect of a manual process.

6. Configuration Management

Usually, the development teams have no view of the infrastructure of the underlying configurations. This results in a huge hurdle where the developer checks in a code that works in the development environment but fails in a higher environment because of its configuration. When you implement configuration management, you automate the management and maintenance of system-wide configurations across networks, servers, applications, storage, and other managed services. This also results in all the environments having identical configurations and enables the development teams with a bigger picture.

7. Application Monitoring

DevOps all about automation and building workflows. A workflow is stitching up a series of tasks to work together. When you start automating, you need to monitor each of these steps, and if that monitoring is going to be done manually, it negates the benefits of having a workflow. Automated monitoring ensures that your workflow is up and running as expected at any time of the day and any number of times it runs. There are two types of monitoring, reactive and proactive. Reactive monitoring capture real-time data and store that data to spot trends. They are generally useful after an issue has occurred. On the other hand, proactive monitoring tools use reactive monitoring tools along with some other capabilities to prevent the issue before it happens.

8. Continous Compliance

Continuous compliance is about achieving compliance and then maintaining compliance on an ongoing basis. While working with your DevOps workflows, a strategy needs to be in place to monitor the compliance at all points in time and trigger a notification if one component fails to adhere to the compliance policies. This is crucial when you want to automate all of your processes and save time during audits.

## CHAPTER SIX

Infrastructure as Code

Infrastructure is the backbone of the software development process, and there are ways to make infrastructure provisioning much more Agile. This is where Infrastructure as Code plays a significant role. As described earlier, Infrastructure as Code is the practice of managing your Infrastructure as a code just like you do for your application code and maintain it in version control. Many tools cater to Infrastructure as code. The tools can be categorised as Declarative or Imperative. The Declarative tool accepts a set of statements that defines the desired state and ensures it is achieved. The Imperative tool establishes a set of commands that needs to be run in a specific order to reach the desired state. The method by which these tools go about their task can fall under Push or Pull. In the pull method, the target server pulls the code from the tool or the server that hosts the tool, and in the push method, the server pushes the code to the target server.

The other aspect of IaC is the ability to save costs when using complex cloud architectures. Since you are billed for use in the cloud model, there are scenarios that specific resources are left behind during clean up and continue to add to your bill. You can terminate all of the resources that IaC provisioned when you ask the IaC to terminate the resource. Similarly, you can recreate the resources anytime you want with an identical configuration. You would not need to login to the cloud console to click several buttons and enter many parameters to provision your stack, all of these can be done just by a single click or by running a few commands.

The following summarises the advantages of using Infrastructure as Code in your DevOps/ SDLC pipeline.

Faster infrastructure provisioning- provisioning infrastructure by running commands or by a single click eliminates the time spent in **the** cloud console and repeated clicks. You can already imagine the kind of time and **effort you**save when you have a significantly complex architecture.

Trustability- You can trust the IaC to provision what you ask it to provision without any **mistakes. In**a repeatable manner. With a large Infrastructure set, it is possible to misconfigure a component or provision the services in the wrong order leading to failure.

Multiple Environments- You can quickly provision environments identical to your production environment, do your testing,and shut it down. You can do this repeatedly, day in and day out,enabling you to experiment and test efficiently.

Best Practices- Writing code to design and deploy infrastructure facilitates best practices without asking your team to perform them. You can also restrict individual groups to use specific kinds of resources.

Auditable- When you use IaC and version control them in a repository like GIT, your entire infrastructure becomes auditable and trackable.

Idempotent - Idempotency ensures that when the same set of codes are applied multiple times, the result remains the same.

There are several tools available that allow you to adopt Infrastructure as Code (IaC). The three cloud providers AWS, Azure,and GCP,also offer you their version of IaC tools. To start with, there is Cloudformation, a service designed for the AWS Cloud. Since AWS remains one of the popular cloud providers on the market today, it makes sense to start your journey with AWS. This could be the most used IaC tool by the developers. CloudFormation allows users to create and edit their infrastructure within a JSON or YAML template file. You only pay for the resources used and not the service itself.

Microsoft offers Azure Resource Manager (ARM) for its users who prefer to use Infrastructure as Code. With Azure Resource Manager, users can provision infrastructure and cater to dependencies seamlessly through templates. The resources are declaratively described within JSON, and you can declare multiple Azure resources in one ARM template.

Google's IaC tool is known as the Google Cloud Deployment Manager. The user can use YAML and templates (JINJA2 or PYTHON) all within the Google Cloud Platform to write the configuration. It makes it possible for you to define the resources and deploy them synchronically. Now comes Terraform, which is not only idempotent, it's the multi-cloud capable and hence also known as swiss army knife of IaC tools. You can use Terraform to manage and provision resources on AWS, Google, Azure, VMware, Openstack, and many more. Terraform is developed by HashiCorp, the same company behind Vault, Nomad, and Consul. Terraform supports the change and provisioning previews and version control and remote states, which provide a centralized source of truth.

Terraform

## CHAPTER SEVEN

Terraform

Terraform is a tool that lets you manage your infrastructure as code. HashiCorp, the company that provides terraform provides many other tools that focus on automation and support applications' development and deployment. HashiCorp defines terraform as follows "Terraform is a tool for building, changing, and versioning infrastructure safely and efficiently. Terraform can manage existing and popular service providers as well as custom in-house solutions." With more and more companies moving towards agile development, the development cycles become shorter, and the releases are made faster. IT managers and engineers have to rely on automation like infrastructure as a code and Terraform to align to this speed.

Usually, when you provision any resource in a cloud environment, you log in to their console, select many options, and enter a few parameters. This may be a multiple-step process in some cases. For a single resource, this may seem perfectly normal. Complex scenarios where you build the entire environment, tear them down once they have served their purpose, and build it again when required, becomes very cumbersome and is error-prone. There is no way to guarantee that the new environment is identical to the old one you created. Terraform solves this problem by allowing you to write a code for your infrastructure so that it can be provisioned and de-provisioned in a repeatable manner. In other words, Terraform gives you a uniform definition of your target infrastructure. Terraform is declarative in the sense that you tell terraform the end goal, and it will make sure you get it. The configuration files are written in HCL (HashiCorp Configuration Language) or JSON, although, using HCL makes your life much better. The configuration file tells the terraform the resources that it needs to create for you. Terraform generates an execution plan that describes what it has to do to get to the desired state and then executes it. If the configuration changes, terraform automatically detects the change and runs a reinitialisation asking you if you would want to migrate to the new configuration.

As technology advances, many companies adopt these technologies to be more efficient and relevant in the market. The current trend is moving towards a hybrid cloud, which means the infrastructure comprises traditional data centres and public clouds. The legacy approach of firing up a console, clicking many buttons, and entering variables are not friendly and is never recommended to manage such a diverse infrastructure. Such a method relies a lot on human intervention and is prone to human errors. Besides, the same steps need to be followed every time the infrastructure has to be provisioned, which uses up a lot of valuable time and effort. What helps in such a situation is to code your infrastructure. This is where Terraform plays a vital role. Engineers used to write scripts and programs to automate many routine tasks, but they were not easily readable by humans. Terraform hands are easy to read and can be grouped into modules for functions that are routinely repeated. It also helps to track changes to your infrastructure and hence enables audit. With Terraform, the infrastructure code and be tested and reviewed before the code is executed. If the results of these tests do not meet our expectations, then it can be rewritten accordingly. Once ready, the code can be used with automation and CI/CD tools, ensuring its repeatability. Often when you have production workloads on the cloud, you want to be as economical as possible. With microservice-based architecture, you can decouple your deployment and applications. With this, you get to take the benefit of the multi-cloud deployment. This helps achieve fault tolerance and takes advantage of various cloud providers' services based on their pricing model. When you reach this stage, you would want it repeatedly and consistently provisioned across multiple cloud providers. This is challenging because each cloud has its API, services, and management plane. Terraform is cloud-agnostic, and a single configuration can be used against multiple cloud providers, which results in simplified management.

Terraform can build infrastructures efficiently because it creates a graph of all the infrastructure components and parallelises the modification and creation of the non-dependent resources.

Key Terraform terminologies and concepts

State: Terraform has a mechanism to map the resources available like virtual machines to what we have specified in our configuration. This information is stored in something called the state. Terraform uses this state to create plans and update the infrastructure.

Module: Modules in terraforming are self-contained packages of Terraform code that can be reused. In other words, if you repeatedly do a set of tasks the same way, then creating a module out of it is the way to go.

Init: Init is used to initialise a working directory that contains terraform configuration code. It downloads the necessary plugins, modules,backend initialisation,and dependencies in the working directory.

Plan: Plan is used to create an execution plan. Terraform performs a refresh and then decides what actions it needs to take to get to the desired state.

Apply: Apply is used to bring the state of the infrastructure to the desired state by performing the necessary changes and updates.

Destroy: Destroy is used to destroy an infrastructure that is managed byTerraform.

Resources: Resources are any virtual component like virtual machines, network, storage, database, etc., that can be part of any cloud. A resource is an infrastructure object that can be managed by Terraform. Whenever terraform encounters a resource block, it sees it as an instruction to control the mentioned resource.

Providers: Almost any infrastructure type can be represented as a resource in Terraform. A provider is tasked with understanding the API interactions and exposing relevant resources. Providers generally are an IaaS.

Taint: Taint marks a Terraform-managed resource as tainted in a state file, forcing it to be destroyed and recreated on the next apply. It does not modify the infrastructure.

Refresh: Refresh finds resources within the state file and identifies drift in the provider outside of Terraform.

Backends

In terraform, a backend determines where a state is stored and how it is loaded. By default, the "local" backend is used,which means that the state file is stored in the local workstation.

Some of the benefits of using a backend are as follows.

- Backends can store their state remotely and protect that state with locks to prevent corruption. This makes it easier for teams to collaborate.
- The state is retrieved from backends on demand and only stored in memory. All sensitive information can be safely put in backends and will not reside in your local disk.
- For more extensive infrastructures applying a terraform configuration will take a long time. Some backends allow the execution to run remotely.

Backends are optional,but they certainly add value in most project scenarios, especially when working as a team.

Providers

Terraform manages resources from multiple cloud providers. Providers within terraform is a component that is responsible for understanding the API interactions for various clouds. There are providers for AWS, Azure, Google Cloud, VMware Cloud, and many more. There is a huge list of providers that have been built by the community too. A provider definition looks like this.

1. *provider "aws" {*
2. *region = "ap-southeast-1"*
3. *alias = "sg"*
4. *}*

In the above case, the provider is for AWS cloud. Terraform associates each resource type with a provider by taking the first word of the resource type name. The arguments between the curly brackets (lines 2 and 3) are configurations that are specific to the cloud provider. In line 3, the alias is used to give the provider a name so that the same provider can be used with different configurations for different resources, for example,creating a VM in other regions. When you run *'terraform init'*, the provider is initialised and installed in the current working directory. Each working directory can have its version of the provider. If you wish to upgrade the provider to the latest version that is acceptable, terraform init provides an upgrade flag.

"*terraform init --upgrade*"

In some cases, you might want to use multiple regions for a cloud platform,and in such cases,you can use the 'alias' attribute within a provider.

"*# The default provider configuration*
provider "aws" {
region = "ap-southeast-1"
}

 # Alternate provider configuration
provider "aws" {
alias = "usa"
region = "us-west-2"
    # To select the alternate provider within
resources

```
    resource "aws_instance" "test" {
provider = aws.usa
# ...
}"
```

Provisioners

Terraform has this concept of provisioners, which can be used for specific nonstandard tasks. You can use provisioners to pass user data or metadata into virtual machines. Provisioners can also be used to run configuration management tools like ansible. However, it cannot model the actions of provisioners as part of the planning stage, mainly because their actions could be diverse and unpredictable. It is recommended to use providers as much as possible over provisioner so that terraform is aware of it and can manage the change.

## CHAPTER EIGHT

Terraform Installation

To run Terraform, you have to set it up in the computer where you wish to run it. It need not be your local computer always. Some enginers prefer to install Terraform on a cloud virtual machine and keep this virtual machine extensively for IaC purposes. Even though the entire concept of infrastructure as code and Terraform sounds daunting, installation is unbelievably simple. Terraform is available as a pre-compiled binary for Windows, Linux,and macOS.

Windows

- Terraform website hosts the terraform Executable File (.exe). You can download the appropriate version by visiting

  https://www.terraform.io/downloads.html

- Once downloaded, extract the downloaded .zip file that contains the terraform executable file.
- Create a new Terraform directory anywhere on your computer and paste the extracted file.
- Copy the **Path**of the executable file

- For ease of use, set an environment variable that points to the **Path**.
- To check if it is installed,open**the** command prompt and type terraform -v,and you should get the current version as the output.

macOS

To install terraform on macOS,Hombrew needs to be installed.

- To install Homebrew, use the below command.

  "% /bin/bash -c "$(curl -fsSL https://raw.githubusercontent.com/Homebrew/ install/master/install.sh)""

- Once Homebrew is installed and works as intended, run the following command to install Terraform.

  "% brew install terraform"

- To confirm the installation, type **terraform**s-v, and you should get the current version as the output.

Linux

- Much like Windows installation, Terraform website also hosts a Linux installer. Download the appropriate terraform zip file by visiting https://www.terraform.io/downloads.html a

- Once downloaded, unzip the folder using the command. If unzip is not installed then you will have to install it prior to running the command below.

  "$ unzip terraform_0.xx.xx_linux_amd64.zip"

- Move the extracted terraform file to /usr/local/bin/ using the command

  "$ sudo mv terraform /usr/local/bin /"

- Confirm the file has been moved and terraform has been installed using the command:

  "$ terraform -v"

Installing Terraform Extension on Visual Studio Code

Althoughmany of you might find it useful **to install**the terraform extension onto **the** visual studio code **directly, this is not compulsory.**Visual Studio Code is **a powerful**text editor and supports all the platforms and can be very easy for developers to get started.

You can download visual studio code from https://code.visualstudio.com/download for Windows, **Linux,** and macOS. Once you have downloaded the visual studio code, **please** open it and go to extension and search for Terraform and Install it. The installation is done, and now you can directly invoke terraform commands from within **the** visual code studio.

Terraform extension in Visual Studio Code

## CHAPTER NINE

Core workflow and terraform cloud

The Core Workflow

Terraform's core workflow is a process around which everything else is stitched. The workflow covers writing the code up to provisioning the infrastructure and various methods of completing this workflow. Typically the workflow as defined in terraform documentation consists of three stages, but I would like to think of it as a four-stage process.

- Write - This is where you author the code in your **favorite**editor.
- Init - Initialize your repository to download the plugins and modules
- Plan - Preview the changes
- Apply - The magical provisioning

Core workflow as an individual

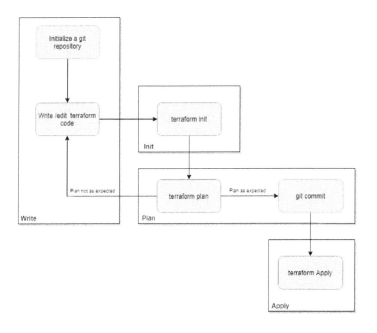

Individual's workflow

While working with Terraform, as an individual, you could work straight out of your laptop. The code is written using your **favorite**editors like Sublime or VS Code. The code will then be checked in a source code repository like git or bitbucket,although this an optional step in this case. You would then run *terraform init* to **initialize**your working directory with the required terraform plugins and modules. The next step is to run the *terraform plan* to generate a detailed plan to show what the code will **finally result in**. While reviewing the plan,if you find something that is not up to the mark, you edit your code again. This process is repeated until you are satisfied with the generated plan. To save this code, you can now commit and push it to the git repository before running **terraforms**apply. Once you run, *terraform apply,* you get one last chance to review the plan before giving your confirmation to provision the infrastructure. Next time you want to make any changes, again repeat this entire workflow. As you can see,the process closely mimics how you write any application code. Hence, infrastructure as Code aptly applies here.

Core workflow as a team

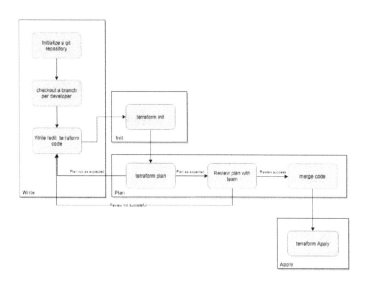

Team's workflow

When you are working with Terraform as a team, the steps within the core workflow changes slightly. The reason for this is that each developer will work on a specific feature (e.g., VPC, Load Balancer, EC2),and all these features need to tie together to create the infrastructure that you desire finally. As in a typical software development process, each of these developers will check out specific branches responsible for and write the configuration. They can individually run *terraform init* and *terraform plans* to see the configuration works as expected and optionally also run *terraform apply*, provided they have access to creating the resources. This allows the developers to test their code, but the developers' codes on different resources have to run together to achieve the end state. For this, the team has to come together and review **the *terraformplan's output***run individually and after merging the code. The review has to be detailed and comprehensive to understand if everything works as expected. Following this review and based on the outcome, ***terraform* can**be run to create the infrastructure.

Terraform cloud

The way terraform works for individuals and teams is slightly different,and with larger teams, this becomes even more complicated. You have to manage a state file so that the teams can collaborate. The state file is a way for Terraform to reconcile what you've created and what you want. Otherwise, Terraform wouldn't know whether to create something or update or delete something that already exists. Terraform cloud is a SaaS environment that manages the state for you,among many other things. When you **run,Terraform the**state file is stored and retrieved from Terraform Cloud. This gives much more control over the state file and lets you see and allow members **to**access it,making it more secure. In addition to that, Terraform Cloud will also version and back up your state file so that you could visualize how your infrastructure was designed in the past.

You can centralize terraform runs to enable all the team members to check the progress and follow the entire process while adding approval steps in **between. You**talk to **the** terraform cloud,and **the** terraform cloud interacts with the cloud. **Every**run that your team has executed will be stored in the terraform cloud. Multiple runs can be queued so that only one run happens at a time.

Core workflow on Terraform cloud

The core **workflow**essentially remains the same **because**you still have to write the configuration and then initialize, plan,and run the configuration. **Always,**with **terraforming**cloud,the plan and run phase **happen**from a centralized location,which enables all the team members **to collaborate effectively**. With the option of adding approvals, **the** team lead can review and approve it on **the**Terraform cloud.

## CHAPTER TEN

Essential commands

While working with Terraform, there is a set of commands that you would be using regularly. These commands form part of the core workflow. Some of these commands are optional, while few others are essential. In this section, we will discuss the following commands

- terraform init: Initialize a Terraform working directory
- terraform validate: Validate a Terraform configuration
- terraform plan: Generate and review an execution plan for Terraform
- terraform apply: Execute changes to infrastructure with Terraform
- terraform destroy: Destroy Terraform managed infrastructure
- terraform fmt: Format the configuration file
- terraform taint: To mark a resource as tainted.

init

The *terraform init* command is used to initialise a working directory containing Terraform configuration files. Init is the first command that is run after writing a new Terraform configuration. This command aims to prepare the working directory for use by Terraform, which includes downloading of the plugins and other initialisation steps. Each time you run the command, it would check and update the working directory, if required. You can initialise the current working directory or any other directory by specifying the directory path while running terraforms init performs the following tasks.

- Download a source module to the working directory: Generally, terraform configuration is already present in the working directory. Another way of initialising an empty directory is to run init with *-from-module=<SOURCE-MODULE-LOCATION>*. This will download or copy the source module into your current working directory.

- Perform backend initialisation: During initialisation terraform checks the root directory for any backend configuration. If a backend configuration exists then, it gets initialised using the provided configuration. If you are running locally, the backend would be configured to use your working directory by default.

- Download other modules that might be required: Terraform searches for module blocks in your configuration files and downloads those modules from the source mentioned as part of the initialisation.

- Download plugins: During init, Terraform searches the configuration for direct and indirect references to providers and downloads the required plugins. For providers distributed by HashiCorp, init will automatically download and install plugins if necessary. Plugins can also be manually installed in the user plugins directory, located at ~/.terraform.d/plugins on most operating systems and %APPDATA%\terraform.d\plugins on Windows.

validate

Terraform validate performs linting of the configuration files in the directory. It only checks if the configuration is syntactically correct and consistent and does not validate providers or state. To perform validation initialised working directory is required. Thus, it is mainly useful for general verification of reusable modules, including the correctness of value types and attributes names.

plan

The terraform plan command is used to create an execution plan. Terraform compares the state file with thereal-world infrastructure and then figures out what actions are required to move the current state to the desired state, as mentioned in the configuration file. The plan is a significant command as it gives you visibility of what change will happen before it happens. It is recommended to run the plan command before making any changes to the configuration and committing the change to version control. You can use the -out argument to save the generated plan to a file, but this file may contain secrets and other confidential data.

apply

The apply command is used to implement the desired state as defined in the configuration file. In other words, it performs a set of actions generated by the terraform plan command. IT usually scans the current working directory for the configuration,or a path to a different configuration file or an execution plan can be provided.

destroy

This command is used to destroy the infrastructure managed by Terraform. You can runthe *terraform plan -destroy command* to check what resources will be destroyed.

fmt

The terraform fmt, or the format command,is used to format the configuration file to a canonical style. Another function of this command is to improve readability. It scans the current directory for configuration files,and if you provide the -recursive flag, it also processes the files within subdirectories.

taint

Taintcommand is used to mark a resource created by Terraform as "tainted". Once a resource is marked as tainted, the next plan will display that the resource will be destroyed and recreated, and the changes occur when the next*terraform apply* is run. Essentially this results in changes in the state files without any change in the infrastructure itself.

## CHAPTER ELEVEN

First Terraform configurtion

Over the last few chapters, we briefly covered AWS, Infrastructure as Code,and Terraform. Now let us see how to use Terraform to provision resources on AWS. The first step is to have an AWS account and create an IAM user with programmatic access.

Step 1: Add User

When you click on Next, AWS would ask you for the policies you wish to assign to the user. Go ahead and add this user to the admin group. If you do not see an 'admin group' in your console, click on the "create group" button to create a group with **the**"AdministratorAccess" policy.

Step 2: Add user to a group

Finally, you can review the configuration for this **user and**create the user.

Step 3: Create the user.

Once the user is created, you will get the required credentials,which are named - Access key ID and Secret access key,which you will have to save as this will be used in the upcoming sessions.

Step 4: Copy the credentials or download the .csv file.

The next step is to download the AWS CLI from https://aws.amazon.com/cli and set it up as per the instructions explicitly provided to the operating system you are using. Once the installation is completed, run the following command to set up your AWS credentials; running this command will ask you for your Access Key ID and Secret Access Key, which you have created in the earlier step. You can access your AWS resources using terraform without any credentials.

"*$ aws configure*"

Now that we have configured everything necessary, let us proceed to create the first Terraform configuration. Create a file called main. tf as shown below

```
provider "aws" {
     region = "ap-southeast-1"
}
resource "aws_instance" "myFirstInstance" {
     ami           = "ami-f546754"
     instance_type = "t2.micro"
}
```

main.tf

In the above configuration, we instruct Terraform to use the AWS provider plugin and mention the region we want our resource to be provisioned. The region ap-southeast-1 corresponds to Singapore. The second part of the configuration uses a resource identified "aws_instance" to create an EC2 instance with a "my First Instance" identifier. There are two other configuration items that we provide terraform.

- Ami - The image from which you want the ec2 instance to be provisioned. You can get this information from the AWS console,depending on the region you select.
- instance_type - The type of instance. t2.micro is the best option if you want to stick to the AWS Free Tier.

Our first terraform configuration is ready, and we can run the '*terraform init*' command to download and initialise the provider plugins.

```
> terraform init

Initializing the backend...

Initializing provider plugins...
- Finding latest version of hashicorp/aws...
- Installing hashicorp/aws v3.22.0...
- Installed hashicorp/aws v3.22.0 (signed by HashiCorp)

Terraform has created a lock file .terraform.lock.hcl to record the provider
selections it made above. Include this file in your version control repository
so that Terraform can guarantee to make the same selections by default when
you run "terraform init" in the future.

Terraform has been successfully initialized!

You may now begin working with Terraform. Try running "terraform plan" to see
any changes that are required for your infrastructure. All Terraform commands
should now work.

If you ever set or change modules or backend configuration for Terraform,
rerun this command to reinitialize your working directory. If you forget, other
commands will detect it and remind you to do so if necessary.
```

terraform init

The next step is to run the '*terraform plan*,' which tells what infrastructure terraform will create. This is an essential step to review and verify if this is the configuration that we require.

```
> terraform plan

An execution plan has been generated and is shown below.
Resource actions are indicated with the following symbols:
  + create

Terraform will perform the following actions:

  # aws_instance.myFirstInstance will be created
  + resource "aws_instance" "myFirstInstance" {
      + ami                          = "ami-00b8d9cb8a7161e41"
      + arn                          = (known after apply)
      + associate_public_ip_address  = (known after apply)
      + availability_zone            = (known after apply)
      + cpu_core_count               = (known after apply)
      + cpu_threads_per_core         = (known after apply)
      + get_password_data            = false
      + host_id                      = (known after apply)
      + id                           = (known after apply)
      + instance_state               = (known after apply)
      + instance_type                = "t2.micro"
      + ipv6_address_count           = (known after apply)
      + ipv6_addresses               = (known after apply)
      + key_name                     = (known after apply)
      + outpost_arn                  = (known after apply)
      + password_data                = (known after apply)
      + placement_group              = (known after apply)
      + primary_network_interface_id = (known after apply)
      + private_dns                  = (known after apply)
      + private_ip                   = (known after apply)
      + public_dns                   = (known after apply)
      + public_ip                    = (known after apply)
      + secondary_private_ips        = (known after apply)
      + security_groups              = (known after apply)
      + source_dest_check            = true
      + subnet_id                    = (known after apply)
      + tenancy                      = (known after apply)
      + volume_tags                  = (known after apply)
      + vpc_security_group_ids       = (known after apply)
```

terraform plan

Once you ensure that the configuration is correct, you can then provision the EC2 machine by running '*terraform apply*'.

```
Plan: 1 to add, 0 to change, 0 to destroy.

Do you want to perform these actions?
  Terraform will perform the actions described above.
  Only 'yes' will be accepted to approve.

  Enter a value: yes

aws_instance.myFirstInstance: Creating...
aws_instance.myFirstInstance: Still creating... [10s elapsed]
aws_instance.myFirstInstance: Still creating... [20s elapsed]
aws_instance.myFirstInstance: Creation complete after 21s [id=i-066fa3b08ede509fb]

Apply complete! Resources: 1 added, 0 changed, 0 destroyed.
```

Terraform apply.

As you can see, the apply command was successful, and one resource was added. You can view the EC2 instance in your AWS console. You can continue using the EC2 instance, or you can clean up using *'terraform destroy'*.

```
Plan: 0 to add, 0 to change, 1 to destroy.

Do you really want to destroy all resources?
  Terraform will destroy all your managed infrastructure, as shown above.
  There is no undo. Only 'yes' will be accepted to confirm.

  Enter a value: yes

aws_instance.myFirstInstance: Destroying... [id=i-066fa3b08ede509fb]
aws_instance.myFirstInstance: Still destroying... [id=i-066fa3b08ede509fb, 10s elapsed]
aws_instance.myFirstInstance: Still destroying... [id=i-066fa3b08ede509fb, 20s elapsed]
aws_instance.myFirstInstance: Still destroying... [id=i-066fa3b08ede509fb, 30s elapsed]
aws_instance.myFirstInstance: Destruction complete after 40s

Destroy complete! Resources: 1 destroyed.
```

terraform destroy

Thus terraform has successfully provisioned and destroyed a virtual machine in Amazon Web Services.

## CHAPTER TWELVE

The State

State in Terraform is a way for Terraform to connect between the configuration and the existing infrastructure, whereas a backend determines how a state is loaded and where it resides. The backend is entirely optional. When terraform creates any infrastructure for you, it has to store all the critical information about the infrastructure to map the configuration files' resources. State also let's terraform track metadata. The state is mandatory for terraform to function. Some people can argue that instead of using state, an alternative like tags could do the mapping. This may be possible, but many cloud resources do not support tagging, and secondly, many resources may have identical tags.

Terraform needs a mechanism to track dependencies as well. The configuration can be used to track the dependency, but what if a dependency has been deleted? Since the configuration no longer mentions this dependency, it is not visible to terraform. For example, if you create a virtual machine with two attached volumes initially and then because the second volume is underutilised, you delete it from the configuration file. In this case, terraform no longer knows that the second volume exists because it has been deleted in the configuration file. Still, the state file would have this information and when comparing the state file with the configuration file, terraform knows what to delete and what to retain. There are other benefits of having a state file that is beyond the scope of this book. Terraform uses the state to create plans and make changes to your infrastructure.

Terraform does a refresh to update the state with the existing infrastructure before doing anything else. The 'terraform refresh' command can be used to do this as well. Refresh can help detect any drift from the last known state and then enable you to make relevant changes. While refresh does not modify the infrastructure itself, it modifies the state file, and if there are changes, then these changes may be triggered when you run 'terraform apply' the next time. State files are also used to cache the attributes of resources, which results in performance improvement. This is mainly done because many cloud providers have API rate limiting, which means that terraform can only request a certain number of resources in a defined time. In such scenarios, the cached state is the source of truth.

State files can also contain sensitive information like database passwords, user passwords, or private keys. In such cases, it is necessary to secure the state file as much as possible. When you store the state file locally, it resides in your disk and is easily readable by anyone who has access to the disk, but a remote state can provide better security using encryption. Secondly, having a remote state will result in Terraform not persist it in the local disk. It is also recommended to track access requests to the state file using auditing tools.

By default, the state is stored in a file named "terraform. state," which resides locally, but it can also be stored remotely, strongly recommended. Terraform can use remote state locking to avoid multiple users running

Terraform simultaneously and ensure that each run begins with the most recent updated state. The following paragraph quickly summarises the purpose of the terraforming state.

Mapping to the Real World: Terraform requires a mechanism to map Terraform configuration to the existing infrastructure because the cloud providers' resource or infrastructure differs significantly. More importantly, every operation needs to be cloud-agnostic.

Metadata: Terraform needs to track various metadata such as dependencies, provider configuration, the order of configuration, etc. This metadata is tracked in the state file.

Performance: Terraform has to keep track of the current state of resources to effectively determine the changes it needs to reach your desired configuration. For more extensive infrastructures, querying every resource is too slow. Terraform stores a cache for all resources in the state.

Team Work: When two or more people are working with the same configuration file, making changes could corrupt the file. Terraform state, with its locking mechanism, helps teams to work together without causing any issues.

State Locking

The idea behind state locking is that no one else should acquire a lock on the state file when a developer is writing to the state file and corrupt it. Terraform takes care of this automatically and silently. One thing to note here is that not all backend supports state locking.

Terraform's state can be managed by'*terraform state*' command. This command's usage is considered quite advanced and typically won't be used when you are just embarking on the terraform journey. Since the state file is a source of truth, management of the state should be done using this method rather than modify the state directly. Some of the necessary commands are listed below.

• terraform state list

This command can be used to list all resources that are found within the state file. You can specify an address, and if you do that, the command will return all the resources that match the address. It will also list resources that are nested within the modules, making the output pretty huge once your infrastructure reaches a certain maturity level. You can optionally filter the state list by resource, by module, and even by ID.

• terraform state show

While the list command lists all the state files' resources, the show command shows a single resource's attributes. This command helps you to deep dive into a resource. You can format the output in JSON by adding a -JSON flag to the command.

• terraform state pull

This command is used to download a state file from a remote location and print it. It also works with local state files.

• terraform state push

Push is used to upload a state file to a remote location manually. This command is rarely used and is not recommended unless manual intervention is required.

- terraform state mv

The move (mv) command can move single or multiple resources within the same or to a different state file as the name suggests. It moves resources from source to destination, which can also be used for renaming, moving resources to modules, or moving a module into another module. Since this changes the state file significantly, a backup is always created.

- terraform state rm

This command is used to remove items from the Terraform state file. The resources are removed from the state file but not physically destroyed, which means Terraform will no longer manage these resources. Like the mv command, you can remove a resource, module, or a resource within a module.

- terraform state replace-provider

The command is useful when you have to replace the source of the provider entirely. You can supply a FROM argument and a TO argument along with the command for this to happen. A backup file is generated before the execution of the command.

## CHAPTER THIRTEEN

Variables: Inputs and Outputs

Variables in Terraform are an essential concept to ensure extensive usage of Infrastructure as Code. In every scenario and use case, you will need to leverage variables extensively to make the code more dynamic. This chapter will help you understand the various options available in Terraform when it comes to variables. In Terraform,the variables can live in a separate file with an extension ".tfvars," ".tfvars.JSON," or only "variables.tf," which makes them easy to understand and edit.

Input Variables

Input variables are used asvalues at run time to customize the configuration. A variable is defined by using a variable block. The variable block has a label that specifies that variable's name and must be unique within a single configuration.

```
variable "ComputerName" {
  type = list
  default = "FirstComputer"
  Description = "Name of the computer"
}
```

List variable type

Any variable declaration can include three arguments, as shown above:

- Type: To specify the kind of value such as string, map, list, etc.
- Description: To explain the variable's purpose so that another user can use it appropriately, much like a readme file.
- Default: To specify a default value to use for the variable. When set, the variable is considered optional. If you want a variable to be mandatory, then leave out the default argument.
- Validation: To define any validation rules if applicable.
- Sensitive: To prevent UI output for sensitive variables.

As seen in the above example, variables in Terraform are defined with the keyword "variable."This is followed by the open curly brackets "{." Inside the block, we can define the type, assign default values, and describe the variable's purpose, followed by ending the block with a closing curly bracket "}."

Types of Input Variables

The type argument functions as an enforcer, allowing you to specify type constraints on the variables. Terraform supports types like string, number, bool, list, map, set, object, tuple, and any. If no type is specified, then Terraform defaults to the type 'any,' which means that any of the available types can be used. Following are the list of variable types availble in Terraform.

- String: A sequence of characters or a word like "Terraform".
- Number: Any numeric value. It can represent whole numbers and fractional values.
- Bool: The boolean value of either true or false.
- List: List is a sequence of values indexed by numbers, starting with 0. The list can accept any value as long as they are all of the same types.
- Map: A map is a collection of values where a key or a string identifies each value.
- Object: Object is a structural type and can consist of different values, but unlike a map or list, each attribute can have its type.

● ◌ ●

```
# string
variable "name" {
  type = "string"
  default = "JohnDoe"
}

# map
variable "ami" {
  type = "map"
  default = {
    ap-southeast-1 = "xyz123"
    ap-southeast-2 = "abc456"
  }
}

# list
variable "az" {
  type = "list"
  default = ["ap-southeast-1", "ap-southeast-2"]
}

# bool
variable "isPresent" {
  default = false
}
```

Examples of variables

Assigning Values to Variables

We have seen how to declare variables, but assigning values to these variables is more useful. There are more than one ways to do that.

- Command Line: Using the command line interface is the easiest way, but it comes with some disadvantages. When you are using either the "plan" or "apply" commands, you have the option to use the flag "-**var.**" You can use as many "-var" flags as variables you have, but if you have many or complex variables in your configuration, it will get very messy, and you may not be able to keep track of it.

> "*$ terraform apply -var="Name=John" -var="Sex=Male"*"

- Variable definition files: If you have many variables and need to assign them values, using the CLI won't be very conducive. Instead, you create a file with the extension ".tfvars" and then past these values with the file would be much more efficient. You can also have a custom name and then point your command to that file, as shown below:

> "*$ terraform apply -var-file="myvarfile.tf"*"

- Environment variables: Environment variables are the dynamic values that are set-up on the operating system itself. Terraform searches for environment variables with a name starting with TF_VAR followed by the name of a variable. This is very useful when it comes to automation. You can create an environment variable for Terraform, as shown below:

> "*$ export TF_VAR_name=john*"

Output Variables

Earlier, we have seen Input variables **that**accept values from the user for terraform to use. Output variables are sent once Terraform completes a run. They can be used by other terraform configuration or any scripts that may need the values from the infrastructure that terraform created, for example, the public IP address of the newly created virtual machine. The output variables can be printed on the CLI when "terraform apply" command is run and individually queried using the command "terraform output". An example of an output block is shown below.

```
output "ids" {
  description = "List of IDs of instances"
  value       = "${module.ec2-instance.id}"
}
```

example output value

The output block name "ids" has been given after using the keyword "output." We then begin and end the block using the opening and closing curly brackets. Inside the block, a particular value has been assigned with an expression that fetches the private_ip for the particular aws_instance.

While "value" is a mandatory field for an output block, we can also have "description," "sensitive," and "depends_on" fields.

- Description: Just like input, output variables can have the description field. It serves the same purpose as documentation.
- Sensitive: If your output variable is some sensitive information such as a password or token information, you may use this field and mark it true. This will prevent it from being printed. However, this information is still stored on "State File."
- Depends_On: Usually, one module's dependency on the other is evident due to the output values. However, by any unlikely chance that the dependency is missed, we can use the depends_on field to determine the dependence.

## CHAPTER FOURTEEN

Modules

A module is a group of multiple resources that are used together. By default, every Terraform script you write has at least one module, known as the root module consisting of all the resources defined within the file. You can write multiple modules, and each of these modules can call other modules. The module called from within another module (parent module) is also called the child module. Modules can also be called multiple times, allowing the creation of underlying resources to be much more readable and user-friendly than having a massive file with thousands of code lines. The idea of having a module is to package a set of resource configurations from a single provider that is required frequently. This allows you to wrap a set of complex configurations that are being used repeatedly within your team or organisation. The usage of modules is recommended for the following reasons:

- When you don't use modules for reusable tasks, navigating the configuration files will become increasingly difficult.
- Updating such configurations may become error-prone as an update in one section may have consequences in some other part of the configuration.

- Without using modules, as your infrastructure grows, there will be an increase in configuration duplication, which confuses.
- It becomes easier to share configurations between teams and projects with modules rather than copy and paste the configuration files.

Modules encapsulate related parts of the configuration together, making it easier to navigate, understand, and update a large project's configuration. It helps a team to organise the configuration into logical units. Another issue that modules address is that you don't have to repeatedly write terraform configurations for the same physical resources for different projects. You can easily reuse one of the modules published by your team members intended for the same purpose. This also ensures consistency and helps to ensure that the best practices are applied across all the projects. Modules can also be stored remotely like in Github or Terraform registry, called remote sources.

Terraform modules are very similar to packages, libraries, or modules found in many other programming languages. There are also certain best practices associated with it, and below is what Hashicorp recommends as the best practices.

- Always write your configuration with modules in mind, even if the configuration is small and managed by a single person. This makes sense because you would start appreciating the benefits that modules bring to the table over a period of time.
- Organise your code as modules, which is not a significant effort but will reduce the efforts when the infrastructure grows. You can use local modules to start

with and slowly and gradually advance on to using remote modules.

- There are a lot of modules already available in public Terraform registry. Use them as your base to get started quickly and confidently.
- When working with a team, it's recommended to publish and share your modules so that others can reuse them.

Terraform Registry

Terraform registry is a web portal with a wide range of modules and providers that you can use in your terraform configurations. It includes modules and providers developed by HashiCorp, vendors, and the terraform community. The portal is available at

https://registry.terraform.io

Screenshot of Terraform Registry

It is effortless to use the portal. You can search for the modules you need, and you get various options to use from. Detailed instructions are provided on how to use the module. In the below image, I have searched for AWS's elastic Kubernetes service.

Terraform module for AWS EKS

The page displayed here for EKS is self-explanatory. It has a Readme section which gives you all the information you need to start with. Some inputs talk about the variables you can define, and the outputs speak about the values you can print out or use as input for other modules. On the top right-hand corner, you would find "Provision Instructions," which you can copy-paste in your local terraform configuration to create an EKS cluster using the default values mentioned in the registry's module. You could also select a different version if you don't want the current version. Terraform registry also gives you examples to study how these modules can be used, and these examples are available for almost all the modules listed in the registry.

## CHAPTER FIFTEEN

Using Modules

When you are working with Terraform, it is perfectly ok to put all the configurations in a single file called main.tf but then it gets very complex, and troubleshooting becomes difficult, especially if there are multiple dependencies. Instead, you could organize them into containers of configurations called modules. Using modules makes your configuration re-usable,as described earlier.

To see the benefits of using modules, you must get your hands dirty. The next few hours should be spent on working the following use-case. Imagine a company called 'Sat Corp' has to deploy an AWS VPC, a database and an EC2 instance. As mentioned previously, there are two options: either put all the configuration in a single file or split them into modules. This works great and is a good starting point. To make it more enterprise-level, repeatable and logical, we can create different folders for each of the resources and then write our main.tf, variables.tf, and outputs.tf within these folders and use a centralized main.tf. In simple terms, this approach can be called as the module drove development.

Let us first look at the folder structure that I have for this lab.

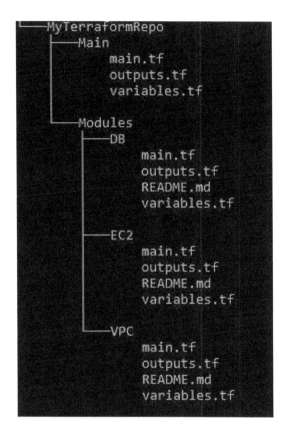

Folder Structure

As you can see in the above image, my main repository is called 'MyTerraformRepo' with two subfolders - 'Main' and 'Modules.'

The Folder Main has three files - main.tf, variables.tf and output.tf. The folder Module has three folders within it, and each of them is for particular resource modules. A folder for a database called 'DB' is a folder for compute called 'EC2' and a folder called 'VPC' for AWS virtual private cloud. Each of these module folders has the same three files as the Main folder - main.tf, variables.tf and output.tf.

Let us look at the Modules to begin with. All the configurations here work with terraform version 0.11

EC2 Module

```
# EC2 Module- main.tf
module "ec2-instance" {
  source                   = "terraform-aws-modules/ec2-instance/aws"
  version                  = "1.19.0"
  instance_count           = "${var.instance_count}"
  ami                      = "${var.ami}"
  instance_type            = "${var.instance_type}"
  name                     = "${var.name}"
  vpc_security_group_ids   = "${var.vpc_security_group_ids}"
  key_name                 = "${var.key_name}"
  subnet_ids               = "${var.subnet_ids}"
  user_data                = "${var.user_data}"
  associate_public_ip_address  = true
  iam_instance_profile = "${var.iam_instance_profile}"

  tags = {
    "tag_environment"  = "${var.tag_environment}"
    "tag_adminname"    = "${var.tag_adminname}"
    "tag_createdby"    = "${var.tag_createdby}"
  }

  root_block_device = [
    {
      volume_size = "${var.root_volume_size}"
      volume_type = "${var.root_volume_type}"
    },
  ]
}
```

main.tf

The main.tf file uses many variables, and the values for these variables are obtained from the variables.tf file. The source points to the terraform registry and the official AWS ec2 instance module. Typically you don't need to create this module and directly call the ec2 module from your configuration file, but I have done this additional step to

illustrate it module works.

```
# EC2 Modules - variables.tf

variable "ami" {
  default     = "ami-0ebf867317f3c5474"
  description = "Amazon Machine ID used for provisioning the instance"
}

variable "instance_type" {
  default     = "t2.micro"
  description = "Type of instance to be provisioned"
}

variable "name" {
  default     = "terraform-instance"
  description = "Assign this name to the instance"
}

variable "iam_instance_profile" {
  default = ""
  description = "IAM role attachment"
}

variable "vpc_security_group_ids" {
  description = "Subnet ID where the instance has to be created"
  type        = "list"
  default = [
    "sg-092dd498120bf0362",
    "sg-c8eca2a9",
  ]
}

variable "user_data" {
  default     = "apt-get update"
  description = "Enter any user data here"
}

variable "instance_count" {
  default     = 1
  description = "Number of amazon instance to be provisioned"
}

variable "key_name" {
  default     = "satish-aws-hpe-seoul"
  description = "Type key to be used for ssh"
}

variable "subnet_ids" {
  type        = "list"
  description = "List of subnets to be associated with the instance"
  default = [
    "subnet-3fbf9879",
    "subnet-656f948e",
  ]
}

variable "root_volume_size" {
  description = "Size of the Root volume"
  default     = 20
}

variable "root_volume_type" {
  description = "Type of the root volume"
  default     = "gp2"
}

// tags
variable "tag_environment" {
  description = "Tag name to be assigned to the instance"
  default     = "dev"
}

variable "tag_adminname" {
  description = "Tag the instance with the admins name"
  default     = "admin@admin.com"
}

variable "tag_createdby" {
  description = "To specify how this instance was created"
  default     = "Terraform"
}
```

variables.tf

A good variable file will describe each of the variables mentioned in the file that describes to any user the usage and purpose of the variable. When you mention the default values, it hardcodes the variable's value and makes it optional. Still, if you don't mention the default value, then that variable becomes a mandatory variable.

```
# EC2 Modules - outputs.tf

output "ids" {
  description = "List of IDs of instances"
  value       = "${module.ec2-instance.id}"
}

output "vpc_security_group_ids" {
  description = "List of VPC security group ids assigned to the instances"
  value       = "${module.ec2-instance.vpc_security_group_ids}"
}

output "tags" {
  description = "List of tags"
  value       = "${module.ec2-instance.tags}"
}

output "instance_id" {
  description = "EC2 instance ID"
  value       = "${module.ec2-instance.id[0]}"
}
```

outputs.tf

Output values in Terraform are similar to the return values in many programming languages. One module can expose components of its resource attributes to another module, using outputs. Outputs act as a bridge between the main and the modules in this case. Similarly, DB and VPC modules too have a main.tf ,variables.tf and outputs.tf. Going back to the folder 'Main' - where you orchestrate all the modules, this becomes relatively easy because you have the modules doing all the heavy lifting.

● ◎ ●

```
# Main - main.tf

module "vpc" {
  source          = "../Modules/VPC"
  tag_environment = "${var.tag_environment}"
  tag_adminname   = "${var.tag_adminname}"
  tag_createdby   = "${var.tag_createdby}"
}

module "db" {
  source                 = "../Modules/DB"
  identifier             = "testprojectdb"
  vpc_security_group_ids = ["${module.vpc.vpc_security_group_ids}"]
  subnet_ids             = ["${module.vpc.intra_subnets}"]
  tag_environment        = "${var.tag_environment}"
  tag_adminname          = "${var.tag_adminname}"
  tag_createdby          = "${var.tag_createdby}"
}

module "ec2_instance" {
  source                 = "../Modules/EC2"
  vpc_security_group_ids = ["${module.vpc.vpc_security_group_ids}"]
  subnet_ids             = ["${module.vpc.intra_subnets}"]
  tag_environment        = "${var.tag_environment}"
  tag_adminname          = "${var.tag_adminname}"
  tag_createdby          = "${var.tag_createdby}"
}
```

main.tf

This looks pretty simple for a configuration file that creates a VPC, a database, and a compute instance. The important part to note here is the "source" parameter that points to the folder 'Module' and the different configuration files. The variables listed here are those that need to be changed on a project to project basis. Also, you can see how some of the output variables are referenced, as shown below.

"*subnet_ids = ["${module.vpc.intra_subnets}"]*"

From the 'Main' folder, if you run 'terraform init,' 'terraform plan' and 'terraform apply,' terraform will pick up the necessary module, run them and create the infrastructure. For each project, you need to have a folder similar to 'Main' and change the configuration file. Any change you make to the modules, the project folders will pick it up automatically when you run the workflow, which makes it reusable.

While working with large projects where you need to create multiple infrastructure components based on your organizational policies, using modules makes it much more manageable. You can easily specify all your organization's policies within the module and ensure that anybody who uses these modules adheres to the policies. Overall, using modules reduces efforts and improves efficiency in the long run.

## CHAPTER SIXTEEN

Terraform cloud and Enterprise

Terraform core workflow that involves writing the code, **initizlising**, **planning,**and running can be done on your local workstation using the Terraform CLI but managing the state file is essential. Also, only a single run at any time is possible. If you want to start a second run, you will have to wait until the first run completes and starts the second one. Managing access control is quite complicated as you will have to do that at the virtual machine level. Finally, approvals are manual where your team members will have to log in to the virtual machine and view the plan or do a screen share and show everyone the plan and get it approved. When working in a team, terraform on a local workstation is fair but not efficient.

Terraform cloud is offered as a service (SaaS or Software as a Service) by HashiCorp. Terraform cloud is a way to execute the Terraform workflow remotely to make it more practical for small and big teams. Some of the features that it offers are

- Remote Terraform Execution: It is vital to have audibility and identical execution environments for any enterprise project. Terraform cloud makes this possible by running Terraform on virtual machines managed by HashiCorp. It also provides a range of other features that you don't have to set up or manage.

- Workspaces: When running Terraform on the local system, you could create folders to manage different infrastructures. These folders will have it on state file, terraform **configuration,**and variables necessary to set up the required infrastructure. In the Terraform cloud, this is achieved using workspaces.
- Remote state management: Your state file can be uploaded to a remote backend, terraform cloud in this **case,**instead of saving it on your local disk.
- The version control system: Terraform cloud can work with your chosen version control system and integrate with it. Each workspace can have it on **the** version control repository with the Terraform configuration. Terraform cloud can monitor the repository for changes and retrieve any change that has is available.
- Private terraform registry: Private terraform registry can help **organizations**to host their modules so that others can reuse them.

In addition to the above points, the Terraform cloud offers various other benefits that users can use to **streamline**their **workflow.**

Summary

Summary

While administrators can create infrastructures manually by using the web console, command line, or shell scripts, it is not always efficient when you have to do these at scale. Using Infrastructure as Code or Terraform can automate and manage the infrastructure with relatively lower risk and improved productivity. For smaller companies or start-ups, developers can take the responsibility of coding their infrastructure and provisioning it as and when they need it.

There are different tools available that can help you to provision your infrastructure like Chef, Saltstack, Puppet or Ansible. How does Terraform differ from these tools, and what benefits does terraform offers? All the tools listed above are configuration management tools that provisions infrastructures based on the changes specified and apply it in-place. Over time, there are a series of applied changes, and it becomes almost impossible for anyone to reproduce it, which results in a configuration drift. With Terraform, each change creates or provisions a new infrastructure rather than change the existing infrastructure.

Using Terraform, you declare the end state you wish to achieve and Terraform makes sure it is achieved. Since Terraform stores information in a state file, it is also aware of all the infrastructure it provisioned earlier, which may not be possible with the other tools. It is common to combine Terraform with Ansible (or Chef, Saltstack and puppet). Terraform can provision all your infrastructure like virtual machines, load balancers, storage etc. and then Ansible can configure and set up your application and database. There are many other ways to use Terraform with these tools, and one can be creative. HashiCorp launched

Policy as Code service by the name Sentinel, which can enforce organisational policies for provisioning infrastructure.

When you start working with Terraform and cloud in general, you will face many different scenarios and situations where one or two tools may not suffice, and you would have to rely on your knowledge on multiple tools and use them in combination to get to the desired state. This book gives you an introduction to Terraform and will help you clear the Associate certificate examination when combined with other resources like the official Terraform documentation.